The

EDINBURGH'S HISTORIC HIGHWAY

Gordon Wright

Steve Savage
LONDON AND EDINBURGH

Steve Savage Publishers Ltd
The Old Truman Brewery
91 Brick Lane
LONDON
E1 6QL

www.savagepublishers.com

Seventh edition published in Great Britain by
Steve Savage Publishers Ltd 2005

First edition 1979
Second edition 1981
Third edition 1984
Fourth edition 1986
Fifth edition 1990
Sixth edition 1997

Text and photographs © Gordon Wright 2005

ISBN-13: 978-1-904246-12-1
ISBN-10: 1-904246-12-5

The photographs on the back cover show: (above) *The Scottish Parliament* and
(below) *A view down the Lawnmarket*
The photograph on the title page shows: *A view down Castlehill*

Map: Malcolm Porter

British Library Cataloguing in Publication Data
A catalogue entry for this book is available from the British Library

Typeset by Gordon Wright
Printed and bound by The Cromwell Press Ltd

INTRODUCTION

In Edinburgh, the greatest concentration of historical interest lies in the stretch of the city which runs down the rocky ridge of land from the Castle to the Palace of Holyroodhouse. This is the Old Town of Edinburgh, the Royal Mile, which has often been compared to the skeleton of a herring, with the Castle the head, the Palace the tail, and the innumerable closes running off the street at right angles, the bones from the spine.

From top to bottom, the Royal Mile incorporates six different sections: the Castle Esplanade, Castlehill, Lawnmarket, High Street, Canongate, and Abbey Strand which leads into the Palace courtyard. The 'Mile' is roughly divided at the junction of the North and South Bridge.

There is so much to see in the Royal Mile that a good guide book is very important and the following pages explain every interesting feature of the past and present, every inch of the way.

If you want to see everything mentioned here, you will need two whole days, and it is with this suggestion in mind that I offer the following plan:

1st Morning: Start at the North Bridge and walk down the left-hand side of the Royal Mile to the Palace of Holyroodhouse. Afternoon: Visit the Scottish Parliament building then explore the other side of the street on the way back up and finish at the South Bridge.

2nd Morning: Start at the South Bridge and walk up the left-hand side of the Royal Mile to Edinburgh Castle. Afternoon: Explore the other side of the street on the way down, finishing your complete tour of the Royal Mile at the North Bridge.

Please remember this is only a suggestion. If you have less time to spare, the times noted in brackets at the main points of interest will be useful in deciding how to make the most of your visit.

Places and landmarks which no longer exist are in brackets.

Numbers refer to the position on the map.

* An asterisk denotes no public access.

A CLOSE is an entry to a tenement, also possibly offering access at the back of the building. At one time there was a gate at the front entrance which was closed at night. Also describes an alley between two buildings.

A WYND is a narrow winding lane.

A COURT is a courtyard surrounded by buildings on all sides.

A LAND is a tenement block of flats.

A PEND is an arched gateway.

Patrick Geddes Heritage Trail

Patrick Geddes (1854–1932) was a lively and most unconventional thinker who travelled the world spreading his ideas on art, science, education, sociology and environmental rehabilitation. His work in conservation and town planning is evident throughout the Royal Mile where each site is identified by a plaque on the wall.

NORTH BRIDGE (1)

The first North Bridge, built on what was formerly the bed of the Nor' Loch, was started in 1763. In 1769, during construction, part of it fell, killing five people. It was opened in 1772, widened in 1876 and taken down in 1896. The iron bridge we see today was started in 1896 and opened in 1897.

CARRUBBER'S CLOSE (2)

The name is probably derived from William de Carriberis, merchant and bailie of Edinburgh, who had his mansion here around 1454. John Spottiswoode, Scots historian and Archbishop of St Andrews (1565–1639) had his house here, and the site is still marked on the right-hand side, although the building was rebuilt in 1864. Spottiswoode crowned King Charles I at Holyrood in 1633 and became Lord Chancellor of Scotland in 1635.

Allan Ramsay the poet (1684–1758) had premises in the close, employed first as a wig-maker and then as a bookseller, and it was from here that he issued a collection of Scots poems *The Ever Green* in 1724, and a play *The Gentle Shepherd* in 1725. Ramsay opened a theatre in the close in November 1736, but the magistrates of the city, influenced by the clergy, closed it the following year, citing the new Theatres Act.

Ramsay's theatre hall was then used by various religious bodies and named the Whitfield Chapel, but by 1858 it was occupied by an atheist club and known as 'The Celebrated Cathedral of the Prince of Darkness'. On 30 May 1858 it was consecrated to the work of the Christian Church once again, when what was to become known as the Carrubber's Close Mission was founded.

In 1865 Sir James Y Simpson (1811–1870), who discovered the anaesthetic power of chloroform, was running a medical dispensary as part of the mission work.

In 1872 the Whitfield Chapel was taken down to make way for Jeffrey Street. At the bottom of the close stands Old St Paul's Episcopal Chapel, built in 1883. The church was founded by

Alexander Rose, Bishop of Edinburgh after the expulsion of Episcopalians from St Giles Cathedral in 1689. The congregation at first worshipped in a wool store at the foot of the close. The church was a stronghold of the Jacobite party in the city and its members suffered accordingly in the risings of 1715 and 1745.

Over the years, Baroness Nairne, ballad-writer; William Edmonstone Aytoun, poet; and Sir Henry Raeburn, RA, have worshipped here.

BISHOP'S CLOSE (3)*

The original residence is said to have been built by Thomas Saintserf or Sydserff (1581–1663), appointed minister in the burgh in 1610 then ordained bishop, successively of Brechin, Galloway and Orkney.

Henry Dundas, Lord Melville, was born at Bishop's Land in 1742. His memorial, the Melville column, can be seen in St Andrew's Square.

During the winter of 1786–87 Robert Burns attended the home of Louis Cauvin Jun. in Bishop's Land where he received three French lessons per week.

NORTH GRAY'S CLOSE (4)

This close is probably named after Alexander Gray, burgess of the city and a member of the great council which met in 1480.

MORRISON'S CLOSE (5)*

This close is identified on Edgar's map of 1742 and recorded in 1750 as having a great house on its east side once owned by John Morrison, merchant.

BAILIE FYFE'S CLOSE (6)

Named after Gilbert Fyfe, merchant and senior bailie of Edinburgh in 1686. Francis Jeffrey (1773–1850), editor of the *Edinburgh Review* and later Scots judge, attended John Cockburn's school here until the age of eight. Nathaniel Gow (1766–1831), son of the famous fiddler and composer Neil Gow (1727–1807), stayed here as a young man, where he taught violin and pianoforte, commanding the highest fees. He occasionally played at the private parties of King George IV. Above the entrance is a shield with what is thought to be the arms of the Yorkshire family of Parley impaled with the arms of Hay and the initials I.P. and M.H. Who they were remains a mystery.

Heave awa' chaps

PAISLEY CLOSE (7)

Named by 1679 after Henry Paisley, who owned property here. On Sunday morning, 24 November 1861, Nos. 99 to 103 High Street tumbled to the ground, killing thirty-five occupants. When rescuers were clearing the debris, a boy called Joseph McIver, trapped beneath the rubble, was heard to shout 'Heave awa' chaps, I'm no dead yet.' Above the entrance to the close a memorial window with an inscription and sculpture of the boy's face commemorates the incident.

CHALMERS' CLOSE (8)

Named after Patrick Chalmers, belt-maker, Captain of the Trained Bands in 1682, who owned a tenement here. Twenty-five years after the old Trinity College Church of 1462 was demolished in 1848 to prepare a site for Waverley Station, the Apse was rebuilt near the bottom of the close as a congregational hall for the new Trinity College Church, built in Jeffrey Street 1872–77. The new church was demolished in the early 1960s but the old Apse was preserved and is now a Brass Rubbing Centre with a fascinating collection of replicas moulded from Pictish stones, rare Scottish brasses, and medieval church brasses.

CARRUBBER'S CHRISTIAN CENTRE (9)

After the demolition of the Whitfield Chapel in Carrubber's Close in 1872, the Mission occupied a variety of temporary accommodation. When Dwight Moody the American evangelist paid a surprise visit to an open-air meeting during his Scottish tour with

Ira Sankey in 1881–82, he was greatly impressed with the work being done. Realising how the work could be extended with suitable accommodation, Mr Moody set himself the task of raising £10,000 for the purchase of a site and the erection of new premises. He succeeded with his ambitious project, and eventually laid the foundation stone of the Carrubber's Close Mission on 24 April 1883. On 4 March 1884 the large hall was opened and two services were held to celebrate the occasion with great crowds in attendance. The Carrubber's Close Mission (now Carrubber's Christian Centre) in the High Street has been active ever since.

Carrubber's Christian Centre

MONTEITH'S CLOSE (10)*

James Kennedy (d.1465) grandson of King Robert III, and counsellor of King James II and III, lived here. He was Bishop of Dunkeld and later St Andrews, where he founded St Salvator's. It is said there was a cachepele or royal tennis court here in the 16th century.

TRUNK'S CLOSE (11)

John Turing, a burgess, had his town house in this close around 1478. 'Trunk' may be a corruption of 'Turing'. After the introduction of a bill to repeal the statutes against Roman Catholics (1779), a house in Trunk's Close supposed to be a chapel was burned down by some rioters. It turned out to be the house of the Popish Bishop. The Cockburn Association, the city's Civic Trust, founded in 1875 and Scottish Book Trust have their headquarters here. The Netherbow Wellhead stands opposite the entrance.

MOUBRAY HOUSE (12)*

Probably dating from 1462, this is one of the oldest houses in Edinburgh, with the popular outside stairway of the period. On the front of the building, a wooden plaque commemorates George Jamesone, the Scottish portrait painter (1588–1644) who once lived here. Jamesone was a pupil of Reubens and a fellow

student of Van Dyck. In 1710, Daniel Defoe (1661–1731), the author of *Robinson Crusoe*, edited the *Edinburgh Courant* from here.

During the 18th century it was a tavern and later the bookshop of Archibald Constable. By 1890 the ground floor had become a shop and the upper floors McLeod's Temperance Hotel. It is now privately owned.

HOPE'S CLOSE AND COURT (13)

Appears as Hope's Close on Ainslie's map of 1780 and was named for the Hope family whose property in the Close was finally sold by Archibald Hope to John Maule, Baron of the Court of the Exchequer in about 1766.

Moubray House dates from the 15th century

JOHN KNOX HOUSE
(14) (20 mins.)

John Knox House

John Knox, who was born in 1513, was originally a priest of the Roman Catholic Church. In 1545 he committed himself to the Protestant faith. With the final struggle for the Reformation in Scotland at the beginning of 1559, its leaders sent for Knox in July of that year and installed him in St Giles as the first minister of Edinburgh. Knox's leadership was an important factor in the events which led to the establishment of the Protestant faith in Scotland and the new forms of worship were shaped through his Book of Common Order. Knox was one of the six who framed the 'Confession of Faith' of 1560 which the Reforming Parliament accepted the same year. Perhaps overshadowed by his work in the Reformation, is the amount of historical documentation which Knox wrote providing an important account of these troubled times. His plans for education in schools and university and provision for the poor were also much to his credit. The house is made up of two traditional houses or 'lands'—a backland dating to the mid-15th century and a foreland which was built around 1472 and then substantially reconstructed in 1556 by James Mossman (goldsmith and keeper of the Royal Mint to Mary, Queen of Scots) who lived here from 1556–72. The result is a most outstanding example of an Edinburgh townhouse of the period. The overhanging wooden upper floors and the crowstep gable end which faces the street are particularly interesting features. The house was subdivided in the late 16th century and an outside stair added. Later the building fell into decay and was damaged when the neighbouring property collapsed in 1839–40. In 1846 it was purchased by the Free Church of Scotland, but in 1849 the Dean of Guild tried to have it demolished to widen the High Street. The public rallied to its defence and saved it from destruction. In 1853, at great expense, the house was renovated and became a museum memorial to John Knox, who may have died here in 1572 when Mossman was besieged in Edinburgh Castle by the Queen's enemies. In 1958 a great deal of restoration was carried out and various features were discovered which had been hidden for centuries. Today, the house is the property of the Church of Scotland and open to the public as part of the Scottish Storytelling Centre.

SCOTTISH STORYTELLING CENTRE (15)

This was once the site of the mansion of the Balmerino family, the last member of which perished on the block in 1746 and the house fell into decay. The Moray-Knox Church also stood on this site until its demolition in 1966. The Netherbow Arts Centre, designed in the style of an old Edinburgh town house, was opened on 19 September 1972 as the Arts Centre of the Church of Scotland. In 2004–05 The Netherbow was incorporated into the new Scottish Storytelling Centre retaining the studio theatre but adding a new educational and welcome area, the Storytelling Court, and the George Mackay Brown Storytelling Library. To commemorate the grouping of these buildings, including John Knox House, around the former Netherbow Port a special contemporary tower has been created incorporating the Netherbow Bell (1621) and the carved stone plaque from the Port. This marks the position of the earliest Netherbow.

BARON MAULE'S CLOSE (16)

Originally Panmure's Close and named after Henry Maule, who purchased a house at the foot of the close in 1711 and became titular Earl of Panmure in 1716. His grandson, John Maule of Inverkeilor, was appointed Baron of the Court of the Exchequer in 1748 and was still resident here in 1773. Hence the current name.

(THE NETHERBOW PORT) (17)

The High Street of Edinburgh ends at the crossroads below the Scottish Storytelling Centre where brass plates inset in the roadway mark the outline of the last Netherbow Port, one of the six gates to the old city of Edinburgh, an arched gateway with tower and spire which could seal the entrance to the city at this point. The original Netherbow Port which was built in 1513 was badly damaged by the Hertford invasion of 1544 but was rebuilt and stood until 1764 when it was demolished allowing a straight passage into the Canongate. The heads of criminals were exhibited on spikes above the gate of the Netherbow, and this must have provided an eerie spectacle for visitors entering the city. The heads of covenanting preachers were also exposed here, stuck up on pikes, between their two hands, the palms displayed as in the attitude of prayer. Lord Wariston's head was displayed with that of his friend James Guthrie, minister of Stirling. In 1745 a party of Jacobites easily captured the gate, allowing Prince Charles Edward Stuart to enter the city.

JEFFREY STREET (18)

Named after Francis, Lord Jeffrey (1773–1850), one of the leaders of the Whig Party. He was Lord Advocate in 1830, MP for Edinburgh in 1832, and Judge of Session in 1834. He was also editor of the *Edinburgh Review* (1803–29). The top part of the curving street we see today was formed in 1872 from Leith Wynd which previously continued in an almost straight line from the junction of the High St and the Canongate downhill to join St Ninian's Row linking it to Leith St and Leith Walk, the main

approach to the Port of Leith. In their premises near the bottom of the old Leith Wynd, the Ballantyne Press printed Walter Scott's Waverley Novels. In 1882, 145,000 copies were published. Scott referred to James Ballantyne as 'a great critic as well as an excellent printer'. Leads to Waverley Station and Princes St.

CANONGATE (19)

The name probably dates from the time when King David I (1124–53) gave the Augustinian canons of Holyrood permission to build on either side of their walk or 'gait' between the Abbey and the Royal Burgh of Edinburgh. The Canongate remained a quiet little burgh until around 1500 when King James IV began to build the grand Palace of Holyroodhouse which became the chief residence of Scottish sovereigns. The Scottish nobility, who wished to have their homes nearby, built fine town houses in the Canongate and the little burgh quickly expanded. Unlike the Burgh of Edinburgh, the Canongate had no protective wall and suffered accordingly during several invasions from the south. After the Union of the Crowns in 1603 the Scottish court moved to London, and following the Union of Parliaments in 1707 and the building of the New Town of Edinburgh around 1767, the Canongate slipped into decline and was eventually absorbed into the Royal Burgh of Edinburgh in 1856. A considerable amount of restoration has taken place in recent years and once again the Canongate has become a desirable district for residence and commerce.

CRANSTON STREET (20)

Shown on the proposed City Improvements 1866, the street was formed beginning at the former entry to Coull's Close and curved westwards to overlie the lower part of Leith Wynd. It was named by 1874 after Robert Cranston, founder of the Cranston Temperance Hotels, then councillor for Canongate, who may have owned ground west of the street, as his son, Lord Provost Robert Cranston, did in 1891. The northern half of the street was suppressed when the Waverley Station goods yard and East Market Street were constructed in the mid-1890s.

CRANSTON HOUSE (21)

Formerly The Canongate Christian Institute (1828–1930), an organisation which ran a mission for the benefit of local people, holding gospel meetings and services several times a week. After lying vacant for many years, it was refurbished and in 1990 became The Edinburgh School of English which teaches English as a foreign language.

MID COMMON CLOSE / MOROCCO LAND (22)*

The story is told of young Andrew Gray, a younger son of the Master of Gray, who, shortly after the accession of Charles I to the throne, was convicted of leading a riot, assaulting the Provost of Edinburgh, and burning his house. Gray was sentenced to death but escaped from the Old Tolbooth jail and disappeared down the Firth of Forth in a boat. Several years later, in 1645, the year of the plague, a large armed vessel appeared in the Firth and docked at Leith. A detachment of the crew approached the Netherbow Port and demanded admission. The manpower of the city was sadly depleted by the effects of the pestilence so the Provost of the city, Sir John Smith, consulted with the most influential citizens to raise a ransom on the town. He returned to the Nether-bow with a group which included his brother-in-law, Sir William Gray, one of the wealthiest citizens. The ransom was agreed, but the leader of the Moors demanded that the son of the Provost should also be surrendered to them. It seems however, that the Provost's only child was a daughter who lay dying of the plague. When the leader realised that the girl was in fact a relation of Sir William Gray, his attitude changed, and he intimated his possession of an elixir

Emperor of Morocco

which would cure her. The girl was carried to the house at the head of the Canongate, and to everyone's surprise, she soon recovered and was returned to her father.

The leader of the Moors turned out to be Andrew Gray, who, after being captured by pirates and sold as a slave, won the favour of the Emperor of Morocco and achieved rank and wealth in his service. He had returned to Scotland to avenge himself on the city magistrates, when, to his surprise, he found in the object of his vengeance a relative of his own. Andrew Gray later married the Provost's daughter and settled down, a wealthy citizen of the Canongate. The site of his house is still marked by an effigy of the Emperor of Morocco which is fixed to the wall above Mid Common Close.

NEW STREET (23)

Built about 1760 and originally called Young Street from the house of Dr Thomas Young. The street was private during this time, with posts and chains, till declared a public street in 1786, but it did in effect remain private until 1819, when it was made a public thoroughfare linking the High Street of the Canongate to the road at the foot of Calton Hill. Henry Home, Lord Kames (1696–1782), judge, philosopher and agriculturist lived here, as did David Dalrymple, Lord Hailes (1726–92), jurist and historian.

BIBLE LAND / SHOEMAKER'S LAND (24)*

185 Canongate is probably called Bible Land due to the sculptured shield over the main doorway showing the first verse of Psalm No. 133. It was here that the cordiners or shoemakers of the Canongate practised their craft, and the shoemaker's arms, the crown and rounding knife of King St Crispin, their patron saint, is also carved on the shield. The gables and bell-shaped termination of the stair tower are notable features of this building. The section adjacent to the Canongate Tolbooth is fairly new, and arcading has been used to give shelter to the footpath. These buildings gained a Saltire Society award for reconstruction in 1958.

GLADSTONE COURT (25)

Named in honour of the Rt Hon William Ewart Gladstone, MP, who became leader of the Liberal Party in 1867. It is listed as Bowling Green Close in 1780 as it gave access to a bowling green. In 1805 the green became the site of the Magdalene Asylum, an institution for 'young girls or fallen women who have deviated from the path of virtue and peace' and became known as Magdalene

Entry. Around 1865 the Asylum moved to Dalry. The Edinburgh Gaslight Co also had premises here, supplying the first gaslight to lamps between the Bridges and Parliament Square in 1820.

OLD TOLBOOTH WYND (26)

The Wynd runs from the passage under the Canongate Tolbooth to join Calton Road at the foot of the hill. John Graham of Claverhouse, Viscount Dundee (1648–1689) usually stayed in the Wynd when he visited Edinburgh. The old Charity Workhouse of the Burgh stood near the foot of the Wynd. It was established by subscription and opened to the poor in 1761. An Old Town well is preserved near the top on the right hand side.

CANONGATE TOLBOOTH / THE PEOPLE'S STORY (27) (20 mins.)

Built in 1591 in the Franco-Scottish style. It was here that the public dues or tolls were collected. At one time it also served as the council house, courtroom and jail of the Burgh of the Canongate, but in 1818 most of the prisoners were transferred to the new jail on Calton Hill. On the front of the building the Latin inscriptions read: 'The place of the seal of the Burgh. For one's country and one's successors, 1591.' and 'King James VI. Justice and Piety are the strong bulwarks of a Prince.' The coat of arms of the Burgh of the Canongate bears a stag's head with a cross between the tynes. The ancient motto attached to the armorial bearing of the Canongate is *Sic itur ad astra*, This is the path to the stars. The outsize clock projecting from the front of the building is dated 1884 and is a replacement of an earlier clock of the 17th century.

The Canongate Tolbooth houses the People's Story

The Canongate Tolbooth now houses The People's Story, an exhibition which recalls the lives and work of ordinary people in Edinburgh from the late 18th century to recent times.

CANONGATE KIRK AND KIRKYARD (28) (20 mins)

The kirk was built in 1688 with funds left by the late Thomas Moodie of Edinburgh for the purpose of providing an additional place of worship for the people of the Burgh of the Canongate who formerly worshipped in the old Parish Church which was in fact from the time of the Reformation, Holyrood Abbey.

Prince Charles Edward Stuart's prisoners from the Battle of Prestonpans in 1745 were confined 'in the Jail and Kirk of the

Canongate'. The Mercat Cross of the Canongate now stands within the kirkyard to the right of the main entrance.

Among the famous people buried in the kirkyard are Adam Smith, the economist; Mrs Agnes McLehose, Robert Burns' 'Clarinda', and Robert Fergusson, the Edinburgh poet (1750–1774), who died in the Edinburgh asylum after injuring his head during an election frolic. Robert Burns was greatly inspired by Fergusson's poems, 'Rhyme I had given up, but meeting with Fergusson's Scotch poems I strung my wildly-sounding, rustic lyre with emulating vigour.' In 1787, Burns paid to have a headstone erected at Fergusson's grave with the following inscription on the back: 'By special grant of the Managers to Robert Burns, who erected this stone, this burial place is to remain ever sacred to the memory of Robert Fergusson.' On the front of the stone is inscribed Burns' own verse:

Statue of poet Robert Fergusson outside the Canongate Kirk

No sculptured Marble here nor pompous lay
No storied Urn nor animated Bust
This simple Stone directs Pale Scotia's way
To pour her Sorrows o'er her Poets Dust.

The bronze sculpture of Fergusson on the pavement near the entrance is by David Annand and was erected by the Friends of Robert Fergusson and unveiled on 17 October 2004.

DUNBAR'S CLOSE (29)

Named after David Dunbar, writer in Edinburgh, who owned the tenements on both sides of the close around 1773. When Burns was in Edinburgh in 1786, a Mrs Love had a celebrated oyster cellar not far from here. It was the sort of place where one could eat and drink and enjoy a country dance to the lively music of a

18

Dunbar's Close Garden

bagpipe or fiddle. Dunbar's Close Garden, donated to the City of Edinburgh by the Mushroom Trust in 1978, is laid out in the character of an Edinburgh 17th-century garden. It is open to the public free of charge and well worth a visit.

PANMURE CLOSE (30)

This close once gave access to Panmure House, the town residence of the Jacobite, James Maule, 4th Earl of Panmure in the early 18th century. The house was later occupied by the Countess of Aberdeen, and from 1778–90 by Adam Smith, the father of political economy. In 1777, Smith was appointed one of the Commissioners of Customs, following the publication of his book *The Wealth of Nations* which argues that every man promotes the interest of his fellows by attending to his own. Adam Smith died in this house in 1790. It is now run as a special club for adolescents and is approached through Little Lochend Close down the street. The poppies above the gate remind us that this close gave access to Lady Haig's Poppy Factory from 1931–65.

LITTLE LOCHEND CLOSE AND LOCHEND CLOSE (31)

The redevelopment of this site in the 1960s has altered the position of the original closes but fortunately preserved the names. The name is derived from James Fergusson of Lochend who owned the house and yard at the foot of the close around 1680. The term 'little' simply distinguishes the narrower of the pair. Behind these buildings is the Calton cemetery, where, near the east wall, rest the ashes of the grandfather, uncle and parents of Robert Louis Stevenson, who wrote:

> There on the sunny frontage of a hill,
> Hard by the house of kings, repose the dead,
> My dead, the ready and the strong of word.

Allan Ramsay wrote an elegy on 'Luckie' Wood, who kept an ale-house in this part of the Canongate. When the Scots Members of Parliament left for London after the Union of Parliaments in 1707, her trade deteriorated drastically.

> O Canigate! puir elrich hole
> What loss, what crosses does thou thole!
> London an' death gars thee look droll,
> An' hing thy heid!

REID'S COURT / CANONGATE MANSE (32)*

Reid's Court is probably named after James Reid, coachmaker, who had lands on the east side of Lochend Close around 1800. The white-walled house, built in 1690, was originally a coaching inn. It served as the Canongate Kirk manse from 1789–1832 and was then utilised by several organisations before falling into disrepair. In 1958 the house was restored and once again is the home of the minister of the Canongate Kirk.

Canongate Kirk Manse

20

Clarinda's Tea Room

CAMPBELL'S CLOSE (33)

Named after George Campbell, meal merchant and bailie of the Canongate, who owned a tenement around 1682 on the north side of the Canongate. In Campbell's Land have resided Arthur Ross, Archbishop of St Andrews, Col George Douglas, later 13th Earl of Morton (d.1738) and James, 14th Earl of Morton (d.1768).

GOLFER'S LAND / BROWN'S CLOSE (34)*

Golfer's Land was a tenement built in the 17th century by bailie John Paterson, a shoemaker, with his winnings from a golf match when he partnered the Duke of York (afterwards King James VII) against two members of an English golf club who were attached to the Duke's court. The bronze coat of arms on the front wall is a copy of a stone carving which was built into Golfer's Land. Brown's Close is named after Andrew Brown who owned property here in the 18th century.

(JENNY HA'S CHANGE HOUSE) (35)

This was a well-known tavern which stood next to Brown's Close from 1600–1857. Janet Hall was the landlady at one time and was famous for her claret which was drawn straight from the butt. Younger's Edinburgh Ale was another favourite, an extremely potent drink which was said to 'glue the drinker's lips together'. It was sold by the bottle and decanted like wine. Allan Ramsay frequented this tavern with many other congenial characters.

FORSYTH'S CLOSE (36)*

Named after Alexander Forsyth, coachmaker and burgess of Edinburgh, who acquired property here in 1719. The Gloucester Gate, named in recognition of HRH Princess Alice, Duchess of Gloucester, patron-in-chief of Whitefoord House, reveals the imposing entrance.

GALLOWAY'S ENTRY / WHITEFOORD HOUSE (37)*

Galloway's Entry was probably named after Alexander Galloway, stabler, who occupied land here in 1804. The Younger Gate gives access to Whitefoord House which was built in 1766 for Sir John Whitefoord of Ballochmyle at a time when the Canongate was the prime residential location in Edinburgh. In 1910 it became a residence for some 240 war veterans who had been living in very difficult circumstances. Today it is a home for Scottish Naval, Military and Air Force veterans.

WHITE HORSE CLOSE (38)

The Royal Mews was situated here in the 16th century. In 1623 Laurence Ord, merchant and burgess of Edinburgh built the White Horse Inn and coaching stables which he named after Queen Mary's white palfrey. It was from the back entrance of the Inn that the stagecoach left for Newcastle and London. When Prince Charlie's army occupied Edinburgh in 1745 and the Prince was in residence at Holyrood, Jacobite officers used the Inn as their headquarters. William Dick (1793–1866), founder of the Edinburgh Veterinary College was born here. The Close was restored in 1965.

(THE GIRTH CROSS) (39)

A radiating circle of cobbles in the middle of the street marks the site of the old Girth Cross. It appears on a map of 1573 as an ornamental shaft elevated on a flight of steps, and was known to be in existence in 1750. Proclamations were made from the Girth Cross and it was the scene of many executions. In 1600 the beautiful young Lady Warriston was decapitated by 'the Maiden' (a guillotine) for conspiring to murder her husband who had cruelly mistreated her. Her maid was also convicted and burned on the Castle Hill.

RUSSELL HOUSE (40)*

A 17th-century tenement preserved by Sir Patrick Geddes (1854–1932). The building was rescued from demolition and restored in 1976 by the perseverence and endeavours of a number of bodies and individuals, including Sir Robert Russell (1890–1972), after whom it is named.

QUEEN MARY'S BATH HOUSE (41)*

Next to the pavement at the north-west corner of the Palace grounds stands a small unusual building which might have been a bath house, a summer house, or simply a doocot (a nesting place for doves).

THE ABBEY STRAND AND SANCTUARY (42)

The Abbey Strand takes its name from the rivulet or strand which once crossed the street here. On the left-hand-side are the 16th-century Abbey Sanctuary buildings which once formed part of a residence for aristocratic debtors. These 'Abbey Lairds' as they were called, were safe from arrest within the confines of the sanctuary which included Holyrood Park and Arthur's Seat and could only safely venture outwith the boundaries on a Sunday. Sanctuary is thought to have existed from the time of the foundation of the Abbey in 1128 until 1880, when imprisonment for debt was abolished. The western portion of the block has been renovated to provide accommodation for palace and court officials.

Abbey Strand: the 16th-century buildings were once home to aristocratic debtors

THE PALACE GATES (43)

At the top of Abbey Strand the large wrought-iron gates, erected in 1922, are part of the National Memorial to King Edward VII. Entrance to the Palace is via the courtyard.

THE ABBEY COURTHOUSE (44)*

The front wall of the Abbey Courthouse retains the outline of the Gothic Porch and Gatehouse which was built in 1502 and spanned part of the present Abbey Strand. The heraldic panel bearing the cypher and arms of King James V displayed on the wall of the Courthouse originally appeared above the entrance to the Gatehouse. The Porch and Gatehouse were demolished by the Keeper of the Palace in 1753. The Abbey Courthouse once housed the Scottish Court. It is now used by the High Constables and Guard of Honour of Holyroodhouse.

THE FOUNTAIN (45)

The fountain in the Palace forecourt was erected at the request of Queen Victoria and the design is based on one made for King James V which stands near the Palace of Linlithgow.

HOLYROOD ABBEY (46)

Legend has it that in 1128, David I, King of Scots, was staying at Edinburgh Castle, and on 14 September after attending mass on the feast of the Exaltation of the Holy Cross, several of his courtiers persuaded him to join a hunting trip. Alwin, an English Austin Canon, the King's Secretary and Confessor, was opposed to the idea, but the royal party ignored his wishes and set off down the hill to the area of forest and stream at the bottom of the present Canongate. During the hunt, a magnificent stag charged the King, throwing him from his horse and pinning him by the thigh. The King tried to grasp the stag's antlers, but found himself holding on to a crucifix which was set between its horns. The King retained the crucifix in his hand while the stag retreated to the spring of water from where it had appeared. During that night, in a dream, the King heard a voice call his name three times, telling him to 'make a house for canons devoted to the cross'. The spring was then called 'the spring of the crucifix', and nearby, the King erected the monastery of the Holy Rood (i.e. cross) and made Alwin the first abbot.

The Abbey flourished, and domestic quarters, an infirmary and a guest house were established within a precinct wall with several gateways. The main entrance faced the castle, and a roadway led to the eastern gate of the town of Edinburgh (later the Netherbow Port). The canons travelled to and fro between the Kirk of St Mary, within the Castle, and the Abbey.

During the revolution of 1688, the Abbey Church was badly damaged and left in a state of disrepair. In 1758 a new roof of stone flags was made but this was badly constructed, and eventually, in 1768, the roof and part of the walls collapsed, leaving the Abbey more or less as we see it today.

THE PALACE OF HOLYROODHOUSE (47) (45mins)

The Palace of Holyroodhouse has developed over the years from a guest house attached to the Abbey to the splendid building we see today. It was King James IV who extended the guest house in 1501 to make himself a royal residence and during the years 1529–32 the north-west tower was built for King James V as a royal apartment. The greatest structural alterations were carried out at the request of King Charles II when Sir William Bruce of Balcaskie, the architect for Holyroodhouse, created the spacious rooms which were built by Robert Mylne, the King's Master Mason between 1671–76. It was during this period of improvement that the south-west tower was built, giving a balance to the front of the palace.

The Palace of Holyroodhouse

The apartments associated with Mary Queen of Scots are situated in the James IV Tower. It was here she received John Knox and where her secretary David Riccio was dragged from her presence and murdered.

The Picture Gallery holds one hundred and eleven portraits of Scottish monarchs by the Dutch artist Jacob de Witt who worked under contract to King Charles II. It was in this gallery that Prince Charles Edward Stuart held assemblies and dances in 1745. It is currently used by the Lord High Commissioner to the General Assembly of the Church of Scotland for his annual banquet.

The first sovereign crowned at Holyrood was James II, and the last was Charles I.

When the Royal family are in residence the Palace is closed to the public.

THE QUEEN'S GALLERY (48) (45mins)

The Holyrood Free Church of Scotland, built on the corner of the Abbey Strand in 1850 (in 1900 it had an active membership of 463) and the adjoining bulding, formerly the Duchess of

Gordon's Free School, were converted and opened on St Andrew's Day, 2002 as The Queen's Gallery.

HORSE WYND (49)

This road once led to the Royal stables. Dugald Stewart, the political economist, had his home 'Lothian Hut' near here.

(HOLYROOD BREWERY) (50)

Beer was brewed in the Canongate from the 12th century when the monks of Holyrood Abbey discovered that the local water made excellent ale. In 1778, on the death of his father, Archibald Younger left the family brewery in Leith and set up business at the northern extremes of the Palace grounds. In 1781, his brother William followed by building a brewery at the bottom of the Canongate. The last brewery on this site was owned by Scottish and Newcastle Breweries Ltd and demolished in 1998 to prepare a site for the Scottish Parliament building.

Clear sightlines in the Scottish Parliament's debating chamber

THE SCOTTISH PARLIAMENT (51)

On 11 September 1997 the people of Scotland voted in a referendum in favour of a devolved Scottish Parliament. The Scotland Act, establishing the Scottish Parliament, was passed by the UK Parliament and received Royal Assent on 19 November 1998. Elections to the new Scottish Parliament were held on 6 May 1999 and the Parliament was reconvened on 12 May 1999 in temporary accommodation in the Church of Scotland Assembly Hall on the Mound. Winifred Ewing MSP had the honour of declaring: 'The Scottish Parliament, adjourned on the twenty-fifth day of March in the year seventeen hundred and seven is hereby reconvened.' An official opening with parade and celebrations throughout Scotland was held on 1 July 1999. On 9 January 1998 it was announced that the new Parliament building would be built at Holyrood. A worldwide competition was held to find a suitable architectural design and on 6 July 1998 it was announced that the Spanish architects Enric Miralles and his wife Benedetta Tagliabue (EMBT) in partnership with RMJM Scotland had been appointed as the architects and designers of the new building. Construction work began on site in April

The 'Canongate Wall' attracts attention

1999. Initially estimated at £40 million in 1999, as work progressed, the cost increased dramatically, resulting in much criticism from the media and the public and heated debate on the Parliament floor. On completion, Scotland's Parliament building cost £431 million. In September 2004 the 129 MSPs moved into their new offices and business commenced. The official opening by HM The Queen took place on Saturday 9 October 2004. There is no doubt that Scotland now has a unique home for its new Parliament. Check at the visitor information desk, inside the front entrance, to find out how you can see the parliament in action or take a guided tour of the building. As you proceed back up the Canongate you will find the 'Canongate Wall'. Various stones from around Scotland are inset here along with quotations from some of Scotland writers. The outline design is based on a sketch by Enric Miralles of the view of the streets he could see from his Edinburgh hotel.

QUEENSBERRY HOUSE (52)

Built in 1651 for Lord Halton, the mansion was later bought by William, 1st Duke of Queensberry (1637–95). The 2nd Duke (1662–1711) accepted a bribe of £12,325 to push through the 1707 Treaty of Union with England which made him very unpopular throughout Scotland. One evening when he was out gathering signatures for the Treaty, his eldest son, Lord Drumlanrig, who was insane, roasted a Canongate spit-boy and was devouring his flesh when his father returned.

In 1745, Jacobite officers wounded at the Battle of Prestonpans were sheltered here. In 1803 it was bought by the Board of Ordnance for barracks. It later became a hospital and old folks home. From 1999–2004 Queensberry House was completely renovated as part of the Scottish Parliament project and now provides office accommodation for the Presiding Officers and their support staff with other facilities.

VALLENCE'S ENTRY (53)

Named after Adam Vallance, barber, who had lands here around 1775. An old town well dated 1817 stands near the entrance.

REID'S CLOSE (54)

Named after Andrew Reid, brewer, bailie of the Canongate, who owned malt barns here in 1770.

DIRLETON HOUSE (55)*

This house, which stands at 84 Canongate, was reconstructed in 1954 as a replica of Sir John Nisbet of Dirleton's house which was built on this site in 1624. Sir John was elevated to the bench in 1664 and made himself very unpopular by dealing out harsh sentences to the Covenanters. Several old inscribed stones are set in the lintel of the present doorway.

ROYAL MILE PRIMARY SCHOOL (56)*

Built in 1888, the school stands in front of the site of Milton House which was built in the early 18th century and derived its name from Andrew Fletcher of Milton, Lord Justice-Clerk of Scotland (1692–1766). Lord Milton was a nephew of the Scottish patriot Andrew Fletcher of Saltoun who tried to prevent the Union of Parliaments in 1707. Milton House was later occupied by a Roman Catholic school, a deaf and dumb school, and the Royal Maternity Hospital before it was demolished.

BULL'S CLOSE (57)

Named after Robert Bull, wright and burgess of Edinburgh, who owned property here in the late 17th century.

CRICHTON'S CLOSE (58)

Named after Alexander Crichton who operated a coachworks here from around 1762 to 1794.

COOPER'S CLOSE (59)

Identified on Edgar's map of 1742, it was named after Richard Cooper, engraver, who trained under John Pine in London but settled in Edinburgh. He was treasurer of the Edinburgh School of Painting etc founded by Alan Ramsay the Elder and others in 1729.

WILSON'S COURT (60)

Named after William Wilson of Soonhope near Peebles, writer in Edinburgh, who feued ground here opposite the church in 1778.

ACHESON HOUSE (61)

Dated 1633, this mansion was built for Sir Archibald Acheson of Glencairney who was appointed one of the Lords of Session shortly after the accession of King Charles I in 1625. In 1628, the King created him a Baronet of Nova Scotia and, later, one of his Secretaries of State for Scotland. On the west side of the house, off Bakehouse Close, is a small courtyard where the Baronet's crest, a cock standing on a trumpet with the motto '*Vigilantibus*', and a cypher containing the initials of Sir Archibald and his wife Dame Margaret Hamilton are set above the door. In 1937, the building was restored, and from 1952–90 it was headquarters of the Scottish Craft Centre. Acheson House is now owned by the City of Edinburgh Council and in conjunction with Huntly House forms the Museum of Edinburgh.

THE MUSEUM OF EDINBURGH / HUNTLY HOUSE (62) (45 mins)

Built in 1570 for John Acheson, the house was occupied by the dowager Duchess of Gordon and her family for a period during the mid-18th century. The projecting upper floors in plastered timber and the three front gables were once very common in the old town. Huntly House was restored in 1932 and is now the main museum of local history in the city. Among the many items of historical interest on view is the National Covenant of 1638 which was signed by men of all ranks as a protest against Charles I's attempt to establish Episcopacy in Scotland and introduce a new service book. There is also a splendid collection of Edinburgh silver and glassware.

The Museum of Edinburgh is in 16th-century Huntly House

Huntly House is also known as 'Speaking House' on account of the four 16th-century plaques displayed on the front of the building. These aphorisms are said to answer criticisms aroused by the splendour of the building. The translations of these, including the 1932 plaque, are as follows.

ANTI QVA / TAMEN / JVVEN ESCO. (I am old, but renew my youth.) The initials are those of Sir Thomas B Whitson, Lord Provost of Edinburgh in 1932 when the building was restored.

HODIE MIHI CRAS TIBI / CVR IGITVR CVRAS / 1570. (Today for me, tomorrow for thee. Why therefore carest thou?)

VT TV LINGVÆ TVÆ / SIC EGO MEAR AVRIV DOMINVS SVM. (As thou art master of thy tongue, so also am I master of my ears.)

CONSTANTI PECTORI / RES MORTALIVM / VMBRA. (The affair of mortals to a steadfast mind is as a shadow.)

SPES / ALTERA / VITÆ. (There is hope of another life.)

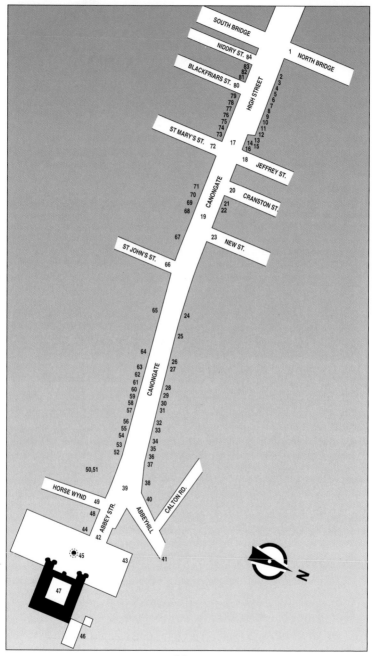

SOUTH BRIDGE

NIDDRY ST. 84

1 NORTH BRIDGE

BLACKFRIARS ST. 80

83
82
81

2
3
4
5
6
7
8
9
10
11
12
13
14
15
16

79
78
77
76
75
74
73

HIGH STREET

ST MARY'S ST. 72

17

18 JEFFREY ST.

CANONGATE

71
70
69
68

20 CRANSTON ST.

21
22

19

67

23 NEW ST.

ST JOHN'S ST. 66

24

65

25

64

26
27

63
62
61
60
59
58
57

CANONGATE

28
29
30
31

56
55
54
53
52

32
33

34
35
36
37

50,51

HORSE WYND

38

39

40

49

ABBEY STR.

ABBEYHILL

CALTON RD.

48

44

42

41

45

43

47

46

N

32

Map of the Royal Mile

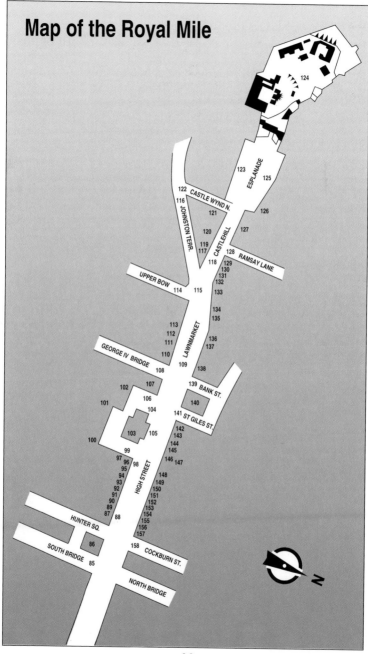

BAKEHOUSE CLOSE (63)

Property on the west side of the close was once owned by the Incorporation of Bakers of the Canongate. In 1851, 230 people were living here. Walk through the close. The back of Huntly House is beautifully preserved. The Royal Fine Art Commission for Scotland is based here offering advice on planning and architectural design with periodic exhibitions open to the public.

SUGARHOUSE CLOSE (64)

This close once led to a sugar refinery. On 24 April 1752 a company was formed which acquired the house formerly occupied by the Earl of Dunkeld. A Charter of Confirmation was granted on 3 June 1767 to the trustees of the Edinburgh Sugar House. David Jardine & Co, sugar refiners, Edinburgh Sugar House, were known to be in operation in 1824.

MORAY HOUSE (65)*

Built in 1628 for Mary Sutton, daughter of Lord Darnley and widow of the 1st Earl of Home, who presented it to her daughter, Margaret, wife of the 4th Earl of Moray. King Charles I was a frequent visitor to the house which had the most beautiful terraced gardens, and Oliver Cromwell had his headquarters here on his first visit to Edinburgh in 1648. On 18 May 1650, shortly after the marriage of Lady Mary Stuart, daughter of the 4th Lord Moray, to Lord Lorne, the chief guests assembled on the balcony facing the Canongate to see the Marquis of Montrose, bound to a

Moray House is now part of the University of Edinburgh

low cart, being taken to Parliament House to receive his death sentence before being hanged at the Mercat Cross on 21 May. Some signatures were appended to the Treaty of Union in the garden of Moray House in 1707. Moray House is now part of a teacher training college, Moray House Institute of Education.

ST JOHN'S PEND / ST JOHN'S STREET (66)

St John's Street was named from St John's Close (c.1780) which was named after the Cross of St John which stood in the High Street of the Canongate and marked one corner of the Temple lands of the Canongate, a triangular enclosure with its apex on St John's Hill. The Knights of St John, members of an ancient order of chivalry had their houses in this district, and today, the Chancery of the Priory of Scotland of the Most Venerable Order of the hospital of St John of Jerusalem is situated at No. 21 in a house built around 1730 for the Wemyss family. In 1989, the fortieth anniversary of its Scottish revival was celebrated and the Cross of St John created in decorative cobblework in the roadway of the Canongate nearby.

Tobias George Smollet (1721–1771) stayed here with his sister, Mrs Telfer, during the summer of 1766 and wrote *Humphrey Clinker* during his visit.

The Masonic Canongate Kilwinning Lodge Hall, built here in 1736, is believed to be the oldest Masonic lodge-room in the world. On 7 December 1786, Robert Burns paid his first visit to the Lodge and on 1 February 1787 he was affiliated as a member. At a meeting in the Lodge on 1 March 1787, the R W Master, Alexander Fergusson of Craigdarroch, advocate, conferred on Burns the title of Poet-Laureate of the Lodge.

OLD PLAYHOUSE CLOSE (67)

In 1746 the foundation of the Canongate Theatre was laid here by Mr John Ryan, a London actor of considerable reputation. Opened in 1747, the theatre was capable of drawing £70 at each performance. The box seats cost half-a-crown and the pit seats one-and-sixpence, and for several years many splendid performances were given in spite of the inevitable opposition of the clergy and other illiberal members of the public. The scene of many a rowdy disturbance, when seats and fittings were ripped up for ammunition, by 1769 the theatre was closed and the proprietor, Mr David Ross, was planning a new theatre to serve the New Town at the east end of Princes Street.

Chessel's Court

CHESSEL'S COURT (68)

Built in 1748 by Archibald Chessel, a wright to trade, who had a seat in the Tron Kirk in 1745. The notorious Deacon Brodie was caught robbing the Excise office here in 1788, convicted and hanged. The buildings which form the façade to the Canongate are a mixture of new and reconstructed 18th-century buildings. The building on the right of the courtyard was originally built as the first real hotel in Scotland. Until then, only primitive inns offered accommodation. The architectural feature of colour wash has been used here and the arcading gives the passer-by an unexpected view of the spacious courtyard at the rear. Restoration was carried out from 1958–67.

PIRRIE'S CLOSE (69)

A William or Alexander Pirrie owned property here at the beginning of the 18th century.

(GIBB'S CLOSE) (70)

Probably named after Robert Gibb, a coach-maker, who owned property here in the early part of the 18th century.

GULLAN'S CLOSE (71)

This close derived its name from James Gullan, stabler, who occupied premises here around 1763–67.

ST MARY'S STREET (72)

Formerly St Mary's Wynd, this street takes its name from a chapel and convent dedicated to the virgin Mary, which included a hospital on the west side at the head of the wynd. These were probably destroyed around 1572.

WORLD'S END CLOSE (73)*

The last close at the bottom of the High Street before the city wall and the world outside. There was once a fish market held here.

TWEEDDALE COURT (74)

The Tweeddale mansion at the back of the court was built for Dame Margaret Kerr, daughter of 1st Earl of Lothian, wife of 7th Lord Hay of Yester and founder of Lady Yester's Church. The mansion later became the Head Office of the British Linen Bank and in 1806, a bank porter called William Begbie was murdered here and robbed of £4,392. The murderer was never caught. In 1817, Oliver & Boyd the publishers took over the building and remained until 1973. The building was restored in the 1980s. The Scottish Poetry Library was first established in the court in 1984 before moving to new premises in Crichton's Close. Canongate Publishers and *The List* magazine are both based here. The original wrought iron gates and a shelter for sedan chairs are very interesting features as you enter.

Tweeddale Mansion

FOUNTAIN CLOSE (75)

Thomas Bassendyne, printer, had his premises in this close and, in 1574, produced the first bible to be printed in Scotland. The name is derived from the fountain or street well which once stood opposite the entrance in the High Street. This well was moved up the street to a position in front of Moubray House in 1813. The Saltire Society have their headquarters here.

HYNDFORD'S CLOSE (76)

James, 2nd Earl of Hyndford had property here in 1710.

SOUTH GRAY'S CLOSE (77)

Named Gray's Close in a charter of 1512 which also mentions a John Gray as a previous owner. It was also the Cunyiehouse Close, from the cunyie house or Royal Mint which was built on its west side near the Cowgate in 1574. The cunyie house was demolished in 1877.

MUSEUM OF CHILDHOOD (78) (45 mins)

Founded in 1955, the museum contains a fascinating collection from Victorian, Edwardian and neo-Georgian times. Although the Museum is mainly intended for adults, and will bring back memories to those who recognise the many items on show here, children will enjoy seeing the dolls, puppets, games, puzzles, hobbies and many other items too numerous to mention. The Museum was extended and reopened in 1986.

TODDRICK'S WYND (79)*

Mentioned as Todrikkis Wynd in Town Council Minutes 1456, its name probably went back to William Tothrik, recorded as owning property here in 1428. In 1685 it was one of the boundaries patrolled by the Town Guard.

BLACKFRIAR'S STREET (80)

Formerly Blackfriar's Wynd which led to the priory of the black or Dominican Friars founded by Alexander II in 1230 on the south side of the Cowgate. On the west side of the street is the former mansion of the Earls of Morton, currently occupied by The High Street Hostel for travellers. The old front door lintel bearing the date 1564 is preserved inside.

The Radisson SAS Hotel which spans Blackfriars St and Niddry St was opened in April 1990 as the Scandic Crown Hotel. It was built to a late 20th-century Scots baronial revival style and the architect was Ian Begg.

(MELROSE CLOSE) (81)

Identified on the front of the hotel. Andrew Durie, Abbot of Melrose from 1528–58, had his mansion in the close.

(CANT'S CLOSE) (82)

Named after the ancient family of Cant, one time owners of Priestfield and the Grange of St Giles, who had their town house here.

(DICKSON'S CLOSE) (83)

Identified above the entrance to the hotel and named after a family who owned land here in the 18th century. One of them, Charles Dickson, was a goldsmith.

NIDDRY STREET (84)

Formerly Niddry's Wynd, it is thought to be named after Robert Niddry, a city magistrate in 1437. The present street is further east than the original due to changes made during the building of the South Bridge.

SOUTH BRIDGE (85)

The South Bridge over the Cowgate, which runs from the High Street to Nicolson Street, was started in 1785 and opened to traffic 11 June 1788. It is 1,075ft long and carried on 19 arches.

THE TRON KIRK / HUNTER SQUARE (86)

The Tron Kirk stands in Hunter Square which was named after Sir James Hunter Blair, Lord Provost of Edinburgh in 1784, who was responsible for the building of the South Bridge. Named after the

tron, or weighing machine, which stood on the site for many years, the kirk was founded in 1637 by order of King Charles I to house a congregation displaced from St Giles's when the royal charter of 1633 made the great church serve as a cathedral. On 16 November 1824, the original wooden spire was burned down, but fortunately the fine hammer beam roof escaped damage and a new stone spire was built in 1828. The Tron Kirk was closed in 1952 and the exterior has since been restored and the foundations excavated to reveal Marlin's Wynd, an old thoroughfare which ran from the High Street to the Cowgate. It is now open thoughout the year as the Old Town Information Centre.

The Tron Kirk stands in Hunter Square, off the High Street

STEVENLAW'S CLOSE (87)

The name goes back to Stephen Law, a flesher, who was made a burgess of Edinburgh in 1501 and had property around here in 1512. He is mentioned in 1537 as the late owner of a tavern or vault in the town.

(EDINBURGH TOWN GUARD) (88)

Edinburgh Town Guard was raised in 1648 and consisted of 60 men and their officers. For many years there were three companies of 1 captain, 1 sergeant, 1 corporal, 1 drummer and 25 privates. A private wore a cocked hat, a rusty-red coat, and a waistcoat and breeches, and was armed with a musket and bayonet during the day and a Lochaber axe at night. The night sentinels were also issued with rattles to attract attention to fire or riot. These foot soldiers were mostly old Highlanders who earned 15s per month for their services. The Guard House was a long, black, slated building of four apartments, one storey in height, which stood in the roadway opposite Stevenlaw's Close. At the west gable there was a wooden horse which drunkards were forced to ride with muskets tied to their feet and a drinking cup on their head, inviting ridicule from all who gathered round. The Guard House was demolished in 1785, and the Town Guard was eventually disbanded in 1817 when they were replaced by a police force.

NEW ASSEMBLY CLOSE (89)*

John Murray of Blackbarony had his mansion at the head of this close around 1580. Later the close led to assembly rooms which were built in 1736 and in use until 1784. The beautiful Georgian building we see today was built by Gillespie Graham in 1814, on the site of the assembly rooms, to house the Commercial Bank of

The Lord Reid Building

Scotland which remained here until 1847. The Royal Scottish Society for the Prevention of Cruelty to Children occupied the building from 1884–1974. In 1975 the building was restored to house a wax museum which was a popular tourist attraction until it closed in 1989. The property is now occupied by the Faculty of Advocates and known as the Lord Reid Building.

BELL'S WYND (90)

Named after John Bell, who had a brewery at the foot of the wynd in 1529. He also owned a tenement at the head of the wynd which was later acquired by the Bishop of Dunkeld.

BURNET'S CLOSE (91)*

Named after Samuel Burnet, a wealthy brewer and prominent citizen of Edinburgh who owned a tenement in the close. He was made a burgess and guild brother in 1591. The Masonic Lodge of Edinburgh (Mary's Chapel) No. 1 met in the Convening House here from 1795–1807.

COVENANT CLOSE (92)*

After the National Covenant was approved in Greyfriars Kirk in 1638, one of the copies was available at a house in this close for public signature. Robert Macqueen, the famous Lord Braxfield (1722–99) lived in this close for a while. He was a judge who struck terror into the hearts of those who appeared before him.

OLD ASSEMBLY CLOSE / TRON SQUARE (93)

There was a tenement built here in 1720 which included an Assembly Hall, which was used for dancing assemblies and fashionable balls. The dances which were held weekly from November to April, continued until 1766 when they were transferred to new premises at 142 High Street (see Assembly Close). The Old Assembly Hall tenement was burned down in the great fire of 1824. Tron Square was built in 1899 and is now largely occupied by the Cowgate Under 5s Centre. An Old Town well stands on the pavement opposite the entrance to the close.

EDINBURGH FESTIVAL FRINGE SOCIETY (94)

Located at 180 High St. Pick up a Festival Fringe programme (published mid-June). Box office: 0131 226 0026.

BORTHWICK'S CLOSE (95)

Named after Lord Borthwick who built a house here in the mid-15th century. It was burnt down in the great fire of 1824. The close leads into Tron Square.

POLICE CENTRE (96)

At 188 High Street, Lothian and Borders police have an information centre with an exhibition tracing the development of the local police force.

OLD FISHMARKET CLOSE (97)

A fish market occupied part of this close as early as 1592 and later there was a poultry market. The close was described as a 'stinking ravine'. The town hangman also lived here. The last of these was a John High who died in 1817. George Heriot, the founder of Heriot's Hospital, lived here for some time as did Daniel Defoe, the author of *Robinson Crusoe*, who acted as a secret agent for the English Government at the time of the union.

SITE OF THE OLD MERCAT CROSS (98)

Near the entrance to Fishmarket Close a cobblestone design in the pavement marks the second site of the Mercat Cross which was demolished in 1756.

THE MERCAT CROSS / PARLIAMENT SQUARE (99)

Enter the Square at the Mercat Cross where royal proclamations are read. First mentioned in a charter dated 1365, the Mercat Cross has occupied five different sites in the course of its history. The present Cross house was erected in 1885 and has part of the original 14th-century Cross built into its shaft. The statue of King Charles II dressed as a Roman emperor, which stands in the centre of the square, was cast in lead in 1685 and is the oldest equestrian statue of its kind in Britain.

DISTRICT COURT, COURT OF SESSION & HIGH COURT (100)*

The District Court on the left-hand side of the square is presided over by a lay Justice. It joins the Court of Session and the High Court, the Supreme Courts in Scotland (presided over by a judge). Sir Walter Scott practised here as an advocate.

PARLIAMENT HALL (101)

Completed in 1639, the hall was occupied by the Scottish Parliament until the Union of 1707. The great hall with its magnificent hammer beam roof, original fireplaces and stained glass windows is now used by lawyers from the adjoining courts who pace the floor as they discuss their affairs with their associates. Adjoining Parliament Hall is the Advocates' Library. There was a Greek frontage added to the hall in 1808, but the original building can still be seen from George IV Bridge. Below the Parliament Hall is the Laigh (low) Parliament Hall which once served Oliver Cromwell as a stable.

Parliament Hall

THE SIGNET LIBRARY (102)*

Pass through the narrow passage to West Parliament Square and the fine building on your left running parallel with the street is the Signet Library with its Upper Hall, which is perhaps the finest piece of interior design in Edinburgh.

The Society of Writers to HM Signet took definite shape in 1594. In 1722 there was a resolution by the Society that Scots law books and statutes be purchased and in 1782–83 flats in Writers Court on the opposite side of the High Street were purchased to form a library. In 1809 the Society decided to participate in a scheme for the erection of buildings in connection with Parliament Hall to obtain accommodation there. In 1815 the new buildings were completed and in 1826 the Upper Hall was purchased and was in use by 1833. On the inauguration of the Chapel of the Knights of the Thistle in 1911, both halls were utilised to assemble the procession and are still used for this purpose today.

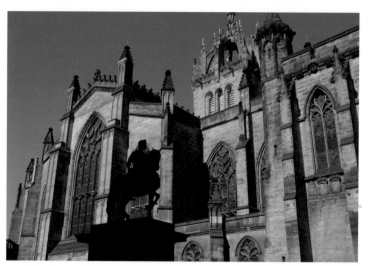

St Giles Cathedral

ST GILES CATHEDRAL: THE HIGH KIRK OF EDINBURGH (103)

St Giles takes its name from a Greek hermit who settled in Provence in the 6th century and became famous throughout Europe. There has been a church here since around AD 854, although the four massive central pillars dating from around 1120 are the oldest parts of the present building. In 1385 the church was burnt by the English during an invasion, but was rebuilt soon after with a stone roof and five chapels. In 1460 the roof was raised, the clerestory windows added and the church extended eastwards. The crown spire was completed in 1495. The Scottish Parliament once met in the Moray Aisle, as did the General Assembly and law courts. A statue of John Knox (d.1572) the great reformer and the first minister of Edinburgh, stands inside the cathedral near the main entrance. When King Charles I introduced bishops to the Presbyterian Church of Scotland, the High Kirk of Edinburgh was elevated to a cathedral. When the 'Glorious Revolution' of 1688 reestablished presbyterianism and the bishop was removed, the title remained. St Giles was restored as a single church in 1883 by Lord Provost Chambers. The Knights of the Thistle, Scotland's chief order of chivalry, had their own chapel built, and this was opened in 1911. Today, St Giles remains a vibrant centre of Christian worship.

THE HEART OF MIDLOTHIAN (THE TOLBOOTH) (104)

The heart-shaped design of cobblestones outside the front door of the High Kirk, next to the road, marks the site of the entrance to the Tolbooth, built in 1561, the base of which is outlined with brass plates in the roadway. Originally a booth for collecting tolls, this was once the meeting place of the Scots Parliament, and also served as Town Hall, chambers for the Privy Council, College of Justice, and after 1640 a prison. There was an annexe of two storeys which projected westwards, and its roof formed a platform for the scaffold. The heads of distinguished victims were displayed on the ornamental north face of the Tolbooth which was demolished in 1817.

(THE LUCKENBOOTHS) (105)

The Luckenbooths (locked booths), built around 1460, were seven timber-fronted tenements from four to six storeys high which were connected to the Old Tolbooth and ran parallel with St Giles, reducing the width of the street to fifteen feet at this point. The shops at street level on the north side sold meat, groceries, bread etc, and most of the merchants had their homes in the flats above along with a variety of professional people.

Between the south wall of the Luckenbooths and the wall of St Giles was a narrow passage called the Krames, where shopless retailers began to offer their wares around 1550–60. The two rows of tiny stands with a narrow footpath running between them sold hardware and leather goods, but mostly a variety of toys and trinkets. Lord Cockburn described it as 'The paradise of childhood'. The first floor of the eastern gable was occupied by Allan Ramsay from 1726, and it was here that he set up the first circulating library in Scotland. In 1786 Ramsay's premises were occupied by William Creech, bookseller and publisher who published the work of Adam Smith, Dugald Stewart, Robert Burns and many other important members of the Edinburgh literati who congregated in his laigh shop to browse and gossip. William Creech died in 1815, two years before the Luckenbooths were demolished.

STATUE OF THE DUKE OF BUCCLEUCH (106)

In West Parliament Square stands the statue of Walter Francis Montagu Douglas Scott, 5th Duke of Buccleuch and 7th Duke of Queensberry KG (1806–84). Unveiled 7 February 1888.

THE CITY OF EDINBURGH COUNCIL CHAMBERS (107)*

Facing the front door of St Giles in West Parliament Square, the original building, erected 1816–18, was called County Hall and built to a design based on a temple in the Acropolis in Athens. In 1892 plans were made for extension and internal rearrangements which involved the entire reconstruction of the west elevation which faces Melbourne Place. The building was also extended to join the Signet Library. The reconstructed building was opened on 26 October 1904. It is now used by the City of Edinburgh Council. An Old Town well stands near the street.

GEORGE IV BRIDGE / MELBOURNE PLACE (108)

George IV Bridge was started in 1827 and completed in 1834, intersecting the Lawnmarket to join Bank Street. It was named in honour of King George IV who visited Edinburgh in 1822. At the south-east corner of the street three brass plates set in the pavement mark the site of the last public execution which was held in 1864 when a murderer called George Bryce was hanged. Melbourne Place, named by 1836 for William Lamb, 2nd Viscount Melbourne, then Prime Minister, identifies the portion of George IV Bridge occupied by the Edinburgh City Council offices which were built in 1968.

LAWNMARKET (109)

The Lawnmarket or land-market, where milk, butter, cheese, vegetables and meat were once displayed on stalls in the street. On Wednesdays a special market for linen and woollen cloth was held. The Lawnmarket starts at St Giles Street and runs up the hill to join Johnston Terrace and Castlehill.

BUCHANAN'S CLOSE (110)*

The name was no doubt connected with Buchanan's Land, burned down in 1771. We have no record of who Buchanan may have been.

BRODIE'S CLOSE (111)

Named after Francis Brodie, wright, glass grinder and burgess of Edinburgh, father of the notorious William Brodie, Deacon of the wrights, respected citizen by day, and burglar by night who was hanged at the Tolbooth on 1 October 1788 along with his accomplice George Smith. Brodie conspired with friends to cheat the hangman by the use of an iron collar concealed beneath his shirt, but the scheme failed and Brodie died. Deacon Brodie was Robert Louis Stevenson's inspiration for *Dr Jekyll and Mr Hyde.*

FISHER'S CLOSE (112)

This building was erected in 1699 by Thomas Fisher, first Chamberlain of Edinburgh. In 1953 the Carnegie UK Trust restored it and reconstructed its interior to provide a home for the Scottish Central Library, which in 1974 merged with the National Library of Scotland. The building now houses a number of administrative departments of the National Library of Scotland, whose main building is in nearby George IV Bridge.

RIDDLE'S CLOSE AND COURT (113)

King James VI attended a great banquet here in 1593, accompanied by his Queen and some Danish nobles. In the courtyard is the house of Bailie McMorran with its peculiar outside wooden stair. Bailie McMorran was killed in 1595 when pupils of the High School rioted over reduced holidays. George Riddell, wright and burgess of Edinburgh rebuilt the foreland here in 1726. David Hume the philosopher (1711–76) lived here before settling in James' Court across the street.

THE UPPER BOW (MAJOR WEIR'S LAND) (114)

The Upper Bow is the top part of the original West Bow which was a southern approach road to the town and castle. At the Bow Head, until 1878, there stood a quaint timber-fronted corner house where Thomas Nelson, bookseller, had his premises. It was in a house off this street that Major Thomas Weir, a native of Lanarkshire came to live with his sister Grizel when, after serving as a major in the Earl of Lanark's regiment, he was appointed to the command of the Edinburgh City Guard in 1649.

Major Weir was a tall man with a grim countenance who wore a dark cloak and always carried a black staff. It was said that this staff had magical powers and ran errands for its master and carried his lantern in the evenings. Major Weir appeared to be devoutly religious, but behind the façade, he was really a despicable hypocrite living a life of perversion and crime. As he approached his 70th year, Major Weir became sick, and summoning some of his neighbours, confessed the most dreadful practices and an allegience to the devil. The city magistrates were informed, but were quite incredulous and reluctant to take him into custody. Eventually Weir was taken to the Tolbooth jail. He was tried on 9 April 1670 when he continued to confess his guilt and was sentenced to be strangled and burned. When he was tied to the stake with the rope around his neck, he was urged to say, 'Lord be merciful to me', but he replied, 'Let me alone, I will not; I have lived as a beast and I must die as a beast.'

His black staff was thrown into the fire with him where it twisted and turned and took a long time to burn.

Grizel Weir was condemned to hang, and at her execution in the Grassmarket of Edinburgh, she struggled to throw off her clothes that, as she expressed it, she might die with all the shame she could. Major Weir's house was demolished in 1878.

(THE WEIGH HOUSE) (115)

The traffic roundabout at the head of the Upper Bow roughly marks the site of the old Weigh House or Butter Tron, where large quantities of butter and cheese were once weighed. It was demolished in 1822 to widen the approach to the castle for the visit of King George IV.

JOHNSTON TERRACE (116)

This is part of the western approach road to the city which was in use by 1836 and was named around 1850 after Sir William Johnston who was Lord Provost of Edinburgh from 1848–51. At No. 1 is St Columba's Free Church which is also the assembly hall of the Free Church of Scotland.

THE HUB (117)

Originally the Tolbooth Kirk, designed by James Gillespie Graham and Augustus W N Pugin. It was built 1842–44 to house the Tolbooth congregation and the General Assembly of

the Church of Scotland. Affectionately known as 'The Highland Kirk', it held regular services in Gaelic. The octagonal Gothic spire, rising to a height of 73 metres, is the tallest in Edinburgh. In June 1981 the congregation moved to Greyfriars Kirk and the church lay empty until it was renovated and opened in July 1999 as the home of the Edinburgh International Festival with a ticket office, restaurant, shop and exhibition space on the ground floor and a performance area and bar on the second floor.

CASTLEHILL (118)

The narrow road connecting the Lawnmarket to the castle esplanade.

BOSWELL'S COURT (119)

A 17th-century tenement named after Dr Boswell, a doctor of medicine, who stayed here around the end of the 18th century. He was the uncle of James Boswell (1740–95), the biographer of Dr Samuel Johnson (1709–84). James Boswell and Dr Johnson are reputed to have met and dined here.

OLD DISTILLERY CLOSE / THE SCOTCH WHISKY HERITAGE CENTRE (120)

Formerly Castlehill School. The close was named as recently as 1997, the name being chosen in a competition between Edinburgh schools. The Scotch Whisky Heritage Centre tells the story of Scotland's national drink through 300 years of the industry's history. A choice of 270 whiskies are available here.

The arrow is pointing at the cannonball

CANNONBALL HOUSE (121)*

Dated 1630, there is a cannonball lodged in the west wall which is traditionally supposed to have been fired from the castle during the Jacobite siege of 1745. In actual fact, it marks the gravitation height of the city's first piped water supply from Comiston Springs to the Castlehill reservoir in 1681, which in turn supplied the old town wells. Cannonball House was until recently an urban studies centre for schoolchildren.

CASTLE WYND NORTH (122)

The steps lead down to Johnston Terrace which runs from the Lawnmarket to the West End of Edinburgh.

THE CASTLE ESPLANADE (SOUTH) (123)

Built in the 19th century as a parade ground for the Castle garrison, it is here that the annual Military Tattoo takes place during the Edinburgh International Festival, attracting 250,000 spectators. Approach the Castle on the left-hand side of the Esplanade and enjoy the view to the south. On the horizon you can see the Royal Observatory on the Blackford Hill and the broad span of the Pentland Hills. The first plaque on the wall is a memorial to David Leslie, Earl of Leven, who raised a regiment of foot in the space of two hours for the defence of the city in 1689. Later titled 25th Edinburgh Regiment of foot, it is now known as the King's Own Scottish Borderers. The second plaque commemorates the officers and men of the Gordon Highlanders and the South African War 1899–1902. The Horse Trough was erected by Princess Louise's Argyllshire Highlanders in 1874.

EDINBURGH CASTLE (124)

Built on a plug of volcanic rock, the castle has provided Edinburgh with a superb fortress throughout the ages, and many an invasion has been successfully repelled. Its history has been recorded since the 11th century and the reign of Malcolm III,

Edinburgh Castle

King of Scots, but fortifications certainly existed from a much earlier date. Cross the drawbridge and see the statues of King Robert the Bruce (1274–1329) on the left, and Sir William Wallace (1270–1305) on the right. Wallace fought long and hard to free Scotland from the domination of the English and died a horrific death in London at the hands of King Edward I.

King Robert the Bruce

Sir William Wallace

Bruce defeated the English army at Bannockburn in 1314 and followed this with a successful campaign. In 1320 the barons of Scotland sent a petition to Pope John XXII which declared: 'So long as there shall be but 100 of us remain alive we will never subject ourselves to the dominion of the English. For it is not glory, it is not riches, neither is it honours, but it is Liberty alone that we fight and contend for, which no honest man will lose but with his life.' A mission to Avignon in 1323 eventually persuaded the Pope to give Bruce the title of King, and at last, in 1328, a satisfactory peace treaty was signed between the Scots and the English.

View from the Castle

Follow the road through Morton's Gateway and the Argyll Tower to the Argyll Battery with its display of cannon and panoramic view over Princes Street to the Firth of Forth. The one o'clock gun which now stands on Mills Mount battery has been fired each weekday since 1851. The Military Prison on the south side of this area was last used in 1923. The adjacent French Prison once held captives from the Napoleonic wars. Follow the roadway through Foog's Gate to St Margaret's Chapel on the top of the hill.

St Margaret's Chapel was built in the 11th century

Built around 1076, this was the private chapel of Margaret, Queen of Scotland, the English Princess who married Malcolm Canmore, King of Scots, in 1069 and it is the oldest building in Edinburgh. Margaret died in the Castle in 1093 shortly after receiving news of Malcolm's death on an English battlefield. Mons Meg, the giant cannon forged at Mons, Flanders in 1449, stands near the entrance to the chapel. It is thought to have been presented to James II by the Duke of Burgundy in 1457. It was taken to the Tower of London in 1758 as a piece of unserviceable equipment, but thanks to the efforts of Sir Walter Scott, it was returned to Edinburgh Castle in 1829. Look over the wall facing Princes Street and see the small graveyard for regimental and soldiers' dogs.

The Half Moon Battery was built in 1574 on the site of David's Tower. Enter Crown Square and find the Crown Room, where the Honours of Scotland, the crown, sceptre, sword and other items of regalia are on display along with the ancient coronation Stone of Scone which was stolen from

Mons Meg

Scotland by Edward I of England in 1296 and returned to Scotland by the British Conservative Government in 1996. The Palace or King's Lodging is where Mary Queen of Scots gave birth to her son, the future King James VI of Scotland and I of England. The Great Hall, built in the early 16th century by James IV, once housed the Scottish Parliament but now contains a display of arms and armour and is occasionally used for receptions and banquets.

The Scottish United Services Museum, opened in 1933, is housed in the old barrack block on the west side of the square which was built in 1707. It is now known as the Queen Anne building restaurant and it has an entrance to the POW exhibition in the old vaults dating back to the American Civil War and the Napoleonic Wars when mostly sailors were imprisoned here.

The Scottish National War Memorial to the soldiers who fell in World War I was designed by Sir Robert Lorimer and inaugurated in 1927. The Shrine holds a casket which contains the names of the dead.

The road back to the Esplanade is via the Lang Stairs. A small plaque on the wall tells how in 1313, the Earl of Moray and a small band of troops climbed the castle rock at night and captured the castle.

THE CASTLE ESPLANADE (NORTH) (125)

A new vehicle access to the castle was built on this side of the Esplanade in 1990. The memorials are as follows:

72nd Duke of Albany's Own Highlanders, Afghanistan War 1878–80.

Ensign Charles Ewart of the Royal North British Dragoons, Battle of Waterloo 1815.

Field Marshall HRH Frederick, Duke of York and Albany, Commander-in-Chief of the British Army in 1827.

The Scottish Horse Regiment, South African War 1901–02. Colonel Kenneth Douglas Mackenzie, 92nd Highlanders.

Earl Haig, Commander-in-Chief of the British Forces, World War I. 78th Highland Regiment, Indian Mutiny 1857–58.

The small well on the eastern corner of the wall marks the spot where, from 1479–1722, over 300 women accused of witchcraft were burned.

RAMSAY GARDENS (126)*

The poet Allan Ramsay (1684–1758) built a house here around 1740, which, from its distinctive octagonal shape was known as 'the Goose Pie'. His son, Alan Ramsay (1713–84), the painter, added a terrace of houses in 1768 and the complex we see today was developed in 1892–5.

(CASTLEHILL RESERVOIR) (127)

The original reservoir of 1681 was replaced by a new system in 1851. It had a capacity of 1.7 million gallons and was fed by various springs in the Pentland Hills. It in turn supplied the high buildings of Princes Street. The reservoir was decommissioned in 1992 and has now been converted into a shopping complex which features a working tartan weaving mill as its centrepiece.

RAMSAY LANE (128)

Leads down to the Mound and Princes Street.

THE OUTLOOK TOWER AND CAMERA OBSCURA (129) (45 mins)

Originally the site of the town mansion of the Laird o' Cockpen. In the 1850s, an optician called Maria Theresa Short purchased the existing building, adding two floors, and installed the Camera Obscura in the tower for an experiment in optics. Sir Patrick Geddes, the pioneer town planner, took over the Outlook Tower in 1891 and converted it into a sociological museum which he operated for several years before transferring his efforts elsewhere. In 1945 a superior lens and mirror system were installed and the Camera Obscura has been in operation ever since. Behind the Outlook Tower is the site of the original ragged school which was founded in 1847 by Dr Thomas Guthrie, preacher and social reformer.

SKINNERS' CLOSE (130)*

In 1635 the Incorporation of the Skinners and Furriers of Edinburgh are recorded as having property here.

SEMPLE'S CLOSE (131)*

The remains of a mansion here bearing the date 1638, prior to 1734, was occupied by Grissel, Lady Semple, widow of Francis, 8th Lord Semple.

The Camera Obscura is in the Outlook Tower

JOLLIE'S CLOSE (132)*

A tenement at the top of the close was owned by Patrick Jollie and later by Alexander Jollie, writer.

CHURCH OF SCOTLAND GENERAL ASSEMBLY HALL (133)*

The hall is built on the site of the Palace of Mary of Guise, Queen of King James V and mother of Mary, Queen of Scots, which was demolished in 1861. The General Assembly of the Church of Scotland, the Supreme Court of the Church of Scotland holds its annual meeting here. From 1999–2004 it was a temporary home for the Scottish Parliament before it moved to Holyrood.

MILNE'S COURT (134)

Designed and built by Robert Mylne in the late 17th-century and one of the first open squares in old Edinburgh, it is now a splendid example of reconstruction and renovation. The court now consists of Edward Salveson Hall, Philip Henman Hall and Patrick Geddes Hall, residential quarters for Edinburgh students.

JAMES' COURT (135)

This courtyard, which has a West, Mid and East entry, was built around 1725–27 by James Brownhill, wright, from whom it takes its name. Around 1790 it started to decline with the rise of the New Town and the original building was destroyed by fire in 1857. It was rebuilt shortly after. Considerable renovation has been completed at the back of the building which now presents a pleasing example of Old Town architecture.

GLADSTONE'S LAND (136)

On 20 December 1617, Thomas Gledstanes, merchant and burgess of Edinburgh, took over property dating from 1550 which he apparently reconstructed and extended to the present six floors and basement. Gledstanes and his wife occupied part of the building and let out four of the flats to a minister, a merchant, a knight and a guild officer. The property remained in the family until well into the 18th century, but was then allowed to deteriorate. In 1934 it was presented to the National Trust for Scotland who renovated it. It is now open to the public as a splendid example of a 17th-century town house.

LADY STAIR'S CLOSE / THE WRITERS' MUSEUM / MAKARS' COURT (137)

The Writers' Museum in Lady Stair's Close

This close takes its name from Lady Stair's House, which was built in 1622 by Sir William Gray (later Lord Gray) of Pittendrum, who married Gidia Smith, sister of Provost Sir John Smith of Groathill. A lintel above the main entrance bears their initials. In 1719 the house was sold to Elizabeth, grand-daughter of Lady Gray, heiress to Sir John Dundas of Newliston, and widow of John, 1st Earl of Stair (1648–1707), and it is after her that the house is named. Lady Stair died in 1731. The Earl of Rosebery acquired the mansion in 1895 and restored it in 1897. He presented it to the City in 1907. It is now the Writers' Museum exhibiting relics of Robert Burns, Sir Walter Scott and Robert Louis Stevenson. In a house on the east side of the close Robert Burns lived during his first visit to Edinburgh in 1786. The courtyard in front of the house commemorates Scotland's prominent literary figures with quotations from their work chiselled into the paving stones.

WARDROP'S COURT (138)

Named after John Wardrop, wright and burgess of Edinburgh, who built a tenement here around 1712.

BANK STREET (139)

Named after the adjacent head office of the Bank of Scotland which was built in 1806. Bank Street joins the Mound leading down to Princes Street.

The High Court of Justiciary

HIGH COURT OF JUSTICIARY (140)

Opened in 1937, this building served as the Sheriff Court House until 1994. Refurbished and reopened in 1997, it now provides additional accommodation for the High Court of Justiciary, the supreme criminal court in Scotland. The bronze statue of David Hume (1711–76), unveiled on 22 June 1997, is by Sandy Stoddart and was financed by the initiative of the Saltire Society.

ST GILES STREET (141)

Built in 1869, it is named from its proximity to St Giles Cathedral, the High Kirk of Edinburgh.

BYRES' CLOSE (142)*

Named after John Byres, merchant burgess (1569–1629), who lived here.

ADVOCATE'S CLOSE (143)

The mansion house of Adam Bothwell (d.1593), Bishop of Orkney, Lord of Session, and Commendator of Holyrood can be seen here. He married Mary, Queen of Scots, to James Hepburn, Lord

Bothwell, 15 May 1567. After Queen Mary's abdication on 24 July 1567, he crowned King James VI at Stirling, 29 July 1567. Sir James Stewart of Goodtrees, Lord Advocate of Scotland, 1692–1709 and 1711–13 also had his house here.

ROXBURGH'S CLOSE (144)

Named after John Roxburgh, a professional cook, who owned property here in 1635. Leads to Roxburgh's Court which connects with Warriston's Close.

WRITERS' COURT LEADING TO WARRISTON'S CLOSE (145)

View of the Scott Monument from Advocate's Close

This court was built by Robert Milne and Patrick Steel, with entry from Warriston's Close around 1690. In 1782 flats were purchased in the court by the Writers to HM Signet to house a library. Alexander Nasmyth, famous for his portraits of Robert Burns, lived here in 1787. This is now the entrance to Mary King's Close.

MARY KING'S CLOSE (146) (1 hour)

Although the lower part of this close was demolished to allow the construction of Cockburn Street which was started in 1859, the paved way and the ground-floor rooms of houses and shops in the upper part of the close along with the adjacent Stewart's Close, Pearson's Close, Allan's Close and Craig's Close still exist under the City Chambers. In 1615 it was known as Alexander King's Close, named after Alexander King of Dryden, prominent as an advocate from 1580 until his death in 1618. In 1629, a woman called Mary King (no relation to Alexander), recently widowed and with four children, rented a house with a cellar and a turnpike (spiral stair) at the top of the close. Mary also rented a small shop in the High Street, trading in fabrics and undertaking work as a seamstress. By all acounts she was well known in the district and did well for herself. Eventually her place of residence became known as Mary King's Close. Mary died in September 1644 just a few months before the great plague devastated the city and most of the inhabitants of the close perished. For some generations after the plague the houses in the close remained closed and gradually it became a place of mystery and horror. It seems a Mr Thomas Coltheart, a respectable law agent, was the first to reoccupy a house in Mary King's close where he and his wife encountered many fearful apparitions. The last known resident of the close was Andrew Chesney, a sawmaker, who was forced out by compulsory purchase and the final tenement was demolished in 1897 to enable the building of the west wing of the City Chambers. Mary King's and the other closes under the City Chambers have now been turned into a popular tourist attraction telling the story of Mary, her neighbours and their way of life in 17th-century Edinburgh. Strange experiences are still being recorded here. Enter by Writers' Court.

EDINBURGH CITY CHAMBERS (147)

Designed by John Adam, the eldest of the Adam brothers, the main part of the building was completed in 1761 as the Royal Exchange and Customs House, but it proved to be unpopular with the merchants of the city who preferred to conduct their business standing in the street. In 1811, the Town Council decided to use part of the building as a Council Chamber, and shortly after, converted the complete building for municipal use. In 1904 a new northwest wing was added.

The 58 members of the City of Edinburgh Council, with the Lord Provost in the chair, meet here to conduct their business, and various other departments operate within its walls. In the forecourt is a statue of Alexander the Great taming his horse

Edinburgh City Chambers

Bucephalus, which was erected in 1916. A plaque on the wall inside the west arch identifies the site of the town house of Sir Simon Preston of Craigmillar, Provost of Edinburgh, and it was here on 15 June 1567 that Mary, Queen of Scots spent her last night in Edinburgh after her surrender to the Confederate Lords at Carberry Hill. The following evening she was conveyed to Holyrood and then to Lochleven Castle as a State prisoner.

Hugh Miller (1802–1856), geologist, naturalist, writer and folklorist, edited *The Witness* newspaper near here at 297 High St from 15 January 1840 until his death in 1856.

(ALLAN'S CLOSE) (148)

The site of this close, closed in 1932, is marked by a plaque on the wall. It was recorded in 1742 but the origin of the name is obscure.

(CRAIG'S CLOSE) (149)

The site of this close, closed in 1932, is marked by a plaque on the wall. Alexander Cant, a prominent merchant burgess, was murdered by his mother-in-law Alison and wife Katherine in his townhouse here in 1535. The two were arrested and condemned to death but Katherine was pregnant and her execution postponed. Alison was put to death by drowning in the Nor' Loch. Katherine eventually escaped to England. Listed in 1742, the close was named after John Craig, wright and burgess who owned property here. Robert Fergusson, Henry Raeburn, Alexander Runciman and Deacon Brodie patronised the Isle of Man Tavern which once stood in the close. *The Scotsman* newspaper opened its first office here in 1816.

(OLD POST OFFICE CLOSE) (150)

The site of this close, closed in 1932, is marked by a plaque on the wall. The close takes its name from Edinburgh's first Post Office which was housed here around 1720. Only one letter-carrier was required to deliver throughout the town. The Wagering Club, founded in 1775, held its first annual meeting here in Matthew Thomson's Tavern.

ANCHOR CLOSE (151)

Named after the Anchor Tavern which was open here from around 1715. Sir Walter Scott's parents lived in the close until 1771. When Robert Burns was in Edinburgh in 1787 supervising the printing of his poems, his printer, William Smellie, who had his premises in the close, introduced him to the members of the Crochallan Fencibles Club who met in the tavern. William Smellie printed the first edition of the *Encyclopaedia Britannica*.

GEDDES' ENTRY (152)*

Named after Robert Geddes of Scotstoun, surgeon, who lived here in the first half of the 18th century.

NORTH FOULIS' CLOSE (153)*

Thought to be named after John Foulis, apothecary, who owned a tenement here in the mid-18th century. At the head of the close James Gillespie (1726–97), tobacco and snuff manufacturer, had a shop. Gillespie was the founder of James Gillespie's hospital and schools.

OLD STAMP OFFICE CLOSE (154)

Named after the Stamp Office which operated from 1779–1821. The Countess of Eglinton and her seven beautiful daughters lived here in the first half of the 18th century. The house later became a tavern where the Lord High Commissioner of 1745 held levees or dances. Flora Macdonald, who helped Charles Edward Stuart escape to France in 1746, attended school here. The New or Royal Bank, constituted in 1727, had its office here until 1753.

LYON'S CLOSE (155)*

Listed in 1742, the origin of the name is obscure. At the bottom of the close is an entry to the old school previously mentioned.

JACKSON'S CLOSE (156)

Probably named after John Jackson who owned property here in the mid-18th century.

FLESHMARKET CLOSE (157)

Named after the flesh market which operated at the bottom of this close in the 18th century. In 1794 a visitor remarked: 'Few cities in Britain are better supplied with butcher meat of all kinds than this city.'

A third-floor flat was occupied by Henry Dundas, Lord Melville (1742–1811) when he first practised as an advocate. The Marrow-Bone Club, whose members were all Whigs, met in Cameron's Tavern.

COCKBURN STREET (158)

In 1853, a company formed by act of Parliament, The Edinburgh Railway Station Access Company, started to buy up lands in the closes which were demolished and the construction of the street started in 1859. It was named after Henry Lord Cockburn, judge, advocate and journalist (1779–1845). Leads to Princes St.

INDEX

Steve Savage Publishers
Books make Ideal Gifts

Greyfriars Bobby: The True Story at Last
by Forbes Macgregor
ISBN 1-904246-00-1 rrp £4.50 illustrated paperback

The Place Names of Edinburgh, by Stuart Harris
ISBN 1-904246-06-0 rrp £24.50 paperback

Lewis: A History of the Island, by Donald Macdonald
ISBN 1-904246-08-7 rrp £12.50 illustrated paperback

Lorimer and the Edinburgh Craft Designers
by Peter Savage
ISBN 1-904246-14-1 rrp £34.50 illustrated paperback

Letters from Hamnavoe, by George Mackay Brown
ISBN 1-904246-01-X rrp £7.50 paperback

Gordon Wright titles:

Rockpools and Daffodils, by George Mackay Brown
ISBN 0-903065-76-2 rrp £14.95 illustrated hardback

Buchan Claik: The Saat an the Glaar o't
A Compendium of Words and Phrases from the North-East of Scotland
by Peter Buchan and David Toulmin
ISBN 0-903065-94-0 rrp £12.50 paperback

A Guide to Holyrood Park and Arthur's Seat
by Gordon Wright, Ian Adams, Michael Scott
ISBN 0-903065-57-6 rrp £2.95 illustrated paperback

Recipes from Scotland, by F Marian McNeill
ISBN 0-903065-79-7 rrp £7.95 illustrated paperback

Scots Proverbs and Rhymes, by Forbes Macgregor
ISBN 0-903065-39-8 rrp £2.25 illustrated paperback

www.savagepublishers.com